NEW PROGRAM IDEAS FOR WOMEN'S GROUPS

Including Five Years of Meeting Plans

Gayle G. Roper

BAKER BOOK HOUSE
Grand Rapids, Michigan

First printing, July 1978
Second printing, July 1979
Third printing, September 1982

PHOTOLITHOPRINTED BY CUSHING - MALLOY, INC.
ANN ARBOR, MICHIGAN, UNITED STATES OF AMERICA

For the women of Calvary Fellowship
—my friends—
with thanks for the material
contained in this book.
You've proved it can work, and work well.

Contents

1. Why a Women's Fellowship? 5
2. A Pattern to Follow 11
3. The Meeting 13
4. A Program of Helps 19
5. Extra Possibilities 23
6. Officers 27
7. Special Programs 35
8. Five Years of Meeting Plans 39

☙1❧
Why a Women's Fellowship?

Judy Reitzel grabbed Leon by his elasticized waistband and pulled him back from the edge of the stairs. With her free hand she toppled a chair and pushed it across the opening.

"We've got to get a gate," she told herself for the hundredth time. "If we don't, this kid's going to kill himself."

"Stay away from there, Leon," she said. "No. No." Judy pointed to the stairs and looked stern.

Leon looked at her, grinned a toothless smile, and immediately began to crawl to the chair. He pulled himself up by its back and tried to raise his short leg high enough to climb over. He couldn't, but already his little bit of movement was pulling the chair away from the stairwell.

"No, Leon!"

Judy picked him up and plopped him in the playpen.

Leon screamed.

"Mommy!" Three-year-old Missy ran into the room. "Mommy, I'm painting."

Judy turned cold. Leaving the safe, though screaming, Leon, she followed Missy to her room. There on the wall that Jim had painted less than two weeks ago was a mural in red and green.

5

"Missy! How could you?"

"I'm painting—like Daddy."

"But he was supposed to. He used ladders and brushes and things."

"I'm supposed to, too. And I used these." Missy extended her hand, and Judy saw with a sinking heart the permanent ink markers that were supposed to be safely hidden in Jim's desk.

"Missy—"

A new and ominous sound reached Judy.

She ran, but she was too late. The dog was already busy being sick all over the new living room shag carpeting. She grabbed the animal mid-gag and tossed him out into the back yard. She returned to survey the damage. What could he have eaten to make him sick?

"Tubby's sick?" Missy asked.

Judy nodded.

"I guess he didn't like the bacon I got out of the refrigerator for him."

"Hey, Mom," shouted a new voice as the front door burst open and whammed into the wall. "I tore my new pants at school today. My teacher wants to see you. And I've got these funny red spots all over me."

Judy obviously needs a night to get out of the house and away from the pressures of her family. It is a legitimate craving she has. To be a better Christian mother she should have time away from her little ones to relax and renew her strength.

Any organization—church, civic, or social—would give Judy her change of venue, but as a Christian, Judy will look to her church. A women's organization merely social in nature will help women like Judy, but there are other women who need more from a women's group. Take Betty.

Betty looked at her husband Paul in distress. They seemed always to be on different sides of every issue.

"Paul, I don't think she should go."

"Look, Betty, it won't hurt her."

"Sure it will. It has to. You know those R-rated movies are no good for anyone, let alone an impressionable fifteen-year-old."

"She's got to learn these things sometime, Betty. Let her go."

"Paul, she's not old enough."

"She looks older. She'll get in with no trouble."

"All that sex and violence. Paul, tell her no."

"You like to go, Betty. You even like the X-rated ones."

"Used to, Paul. Used to. Now that I'm a Christian I can't stomach them."

"Christian-smistian. I'm not going to stop her, Betty. You can try to if you want."

Betty has very different needs than Judy. Betty's children are older, and her husband is not a Christian. Betty needs to talk to and be with Christian women. She needs to be supported and encouraged by those who understand what she's trying to do and who sympathize when she faces obstacles. No civic or social organization can give Betty the necessary sustenance. Only prayers, concern, and love from Christian sisters can do that.

However handholding and sympathy are not reasons enough for having a women's group.

Lydia watched her neighbor walk home. She felt frustrated because she hadn't been able to express herself as she wanted.

"Have you ever prayed about it?" she had asked her neighbor Polly.

"Come on, Lydia. God's got more important things on His mind than my George's job."

"No. He doesn't."

"You mean that world peace and hunger and all that sort of thing aren't more important than George and his new job?"

"Well, sure they are in a way, but God cares about all our problems."

"I'm sorry, Lydia, but I couldn't possibly bother God about something so insignificant in the scheme of things as George's job."

As Lydia watched Polly walk home, she knew that she, not Polly, was right about God's attitude. God did care about George and his job. The trouble was that Lydia couldn't back up her feeling with proof. There had to be verses in the Bible somewhere that said God cared. She just didn't know where. There was so much to learn now that she was a Christian.

Lydia is a young Christian with one basic problem: lack of knowledge. A women's fellowship will meet her needs by teaching her something, by instructing her in the Word, by giving her answers for the spiritual blanks in her life.

But instruction won't help Rhoda.

Rhoda rested her head against the back of the car seat. She was tired to the core of her being. She hoped she could hold together until Joe's illness was resolved one way or the other.

She took a deep breath and sat up. She forced herself to drive home, stopping at Aunt Esther's for the kids. She tried to put down her guilt for the small amount of time she spent with them.

Getting out of the car at her own front curb, Rhoda felt only dread at facing the kitchen. Dinner seemed a chore beyond her abilities. She stumbled up the walk, tripping on an uneven flagstone.

Joe wouldn't have let the stone stay loose. He would have fixed it right away. Rhoda had neither the time nor the energy to repair the hazards. Her part-time job (hospitalization was so expensive!), the kids, Joe, the house—there was no time for wobbly flagstones.

"Hey, Mom, look!" Joey pointed to the step. "Someone's been here."

A basket sat there, a note taped to its handle.

Rhoda,
I hope you like spaghetti. I'll stop for the dishes tomorrow. Just leave them on the step like this. Can I have Joey and Marie overnight Friday? I'll pick them up at school. You can stop for them on your way home from the hospital Saturday night.
Joe's in our prayers.

Barb

"Spaghetti!" Joey rummaged through the basket. "And salad. And apple pie. And paper plates and cups. There's even sodas for me and Marie. The only thing missing is your coffee, Mom."

Rhoda felt vast relief. Nothing to do from now until 6:30 and the trip back to see Joe but eat, relax, and be with the kids. And she would be able to sleep in Saturday.

The flagstone rocked again under Rhoda, but the world seemed much firmer.

A balanced women's fellowship must strive to meet the needs of all four of these women: Judy, Betty, Lydia, and Rhoda—and the countless others with similar problems. To do this, a group must offer revitalization, support, instruction, and practical help.

Without revitalization and relaxation, a group becomes humorless and prim. "But they that wait upon the Lord shall renew their strength . . ." (Isa. 40:31).

If a group doesn't offer support, it becomes selfish and critical. "Bear ye one another's burdens, and so fulfill the law of Christ" (Gal. 6:2).

Without instruction, a group becomes shallow and whimsical. ". . . give attendance to reading, to exhortation, to doctrine" (I Tim. 4:13).

A group becomes smug and heartless if it doesn't offer practical help to those with trouble. "Even so faith, if it hath not works, is dead, being alone" (James 2:17).

A Pattern
to Follow

Discussing how to pattern a women's program makes me think of the school talent show.

"I want to be in the show, Mom," said seven-year-old Jeff.

"Fine. What are you going to do?"

"I don't know. What's my talent?"

"If you have to ask, honey, maybe we should forget about it."

"But, Mom, Chip's in it." Chip is nine.

"True."

"He sang."

"Can you sing?"

"I don't think so," answered my boy soprano who is so soft-spoken that I can't even hear him from the back seat of the car.

"I don't think so either. You know, honey, I think you'd better sit this one out."

"But I want to be in it."

"I know. But if we can't figure out what you can do, maybe we'd better wait until next year."

"Guess what, Dad," Jeff says at dinner. "Mom won't let me be in the talent show."

The whole discussion between my son and me revolved around the issue of pattern, though I'm certain Jeff didn't realize it. Jeff wanted to follow his brother's example. Chip had set the pattern by being in the show, and Jeff wanted to follow suit even if he wasn't able. Convincing Jeff that he is different from Chip is my ofttimes thankless but highly necessary task. No two kids, even brothers, follow the same pattern of development.

The same idea applies to patterning a women's group. I'm going to place before you some highly profitable models and suggestions. They may or may not fit your specific situation. Patterns are never ironclad. Principles are. The principles of Chapter 1 must be incorporated into your group. The patterns that follow should be read, considered, and then applied to fit your needs. I've seen them work, and work well, but they are only patterns.

If you can be in the talent show, fine. If not, adapt, adjust. Be creative. In patterning your imagination is your only limit.

3

The Meeting

The basic ingredient for a church's women's group is the monthly meeting. Since this meeting is what attracts the women and holds them in the group, much thought and prayer must go into the planning of each of its four phases.

The Speaker

When you invite a speaker to your meeting, don't invite someone just to have a person who talks. Look for someone who has something of spiritual value to say.

Look in your own group. Probably you have two or three or more built-in speakers. Recently at one of our meetings, Linda and Eileen shared stories of the adoption of their children. Last year Laura, Kay, and Angela shared a meeting on the theme of faith. It was fascinating to see our own friends in this new light, and we were blessed by the depth of truth that they shared. (They are all homemakers.)

Probably though, many if not most of your speakers will come from outside your church. Look around your community, your county. There will be many fine speakers within this radius. Ask different types of speakers: old or young, vibrant and outgoing or quiet and thoughtful, full-time Christian workers or "regular" Christians. They don't have to be Bible scholars. After all, we're not competing with the Sunday services. But each speaker does need to know Christ in a real and personal way.

Don't be afraid to ask "big name" speakers. They are usually willing to visit any group regardless of size. If you can't pay them much, tell them. It probably will not matter.

Consider going outside your own denomination or association of churches. Obviously a group of Baptists shouldn't ask the Presbyterian minister's wife to speak on baptism and expect to be happy with her presentation. But she can speak on how she became a Christian, or on a topic such as faith, or on what she feels is the greatest challenge facing Christian women today. The verities of Scripture cross many lines.

Certainly there will be some personalities whom you will not want to talk to your group, some with whom you have grave differences. To prevent any problems have all prospective speakers approved by your church board. This one action does much to protect both the officers of your group and the doctrinal stand of your church. The board is our buffer against wolves in sheep's clothing.

In short, be creative but selective, in your choice of speakers. Reach out but be circumspect. On the shoulders of this person rests, to a large extent, the success or failure of your meeting.

The Craft Demonstration

A craft demonstration at your church meeting? Yes, most definitely. While the speaker rekindles our spiritual fires, the craft demonstration challenges us to make our temporal existence more interesting and stimulating. Watching Christian women explain the various creative outlets they have discovered broadens our view of what we can become. We become not merely women, but creative beings accomplishing something of beauty.

Since Norma showed our group how to make occasional wreaths, our front doors are abloom all year long.

Since Mary demonstrated her dough art, our Christmas trees bend beneath dough ornaments and our walls are hung with dough plaques.

Since Shirley told us how to do sand sculpture, our terrariums are based on elegant sand drawings.

Obviously not everyone goes home and does every craft. There may be neither time, talent, nor inclination. But each month creativity raises its gauntlet and slaps us on the cheek. The challenge cannot be ignored. Whatever ability God has given us is re-examined and used more fully.

Aside from the personal enrichment of crafts, they serve as a drawing card.

"Sally, I know you like flower arranging. We're having a florist come to our women's meeting next Tuesday to show us how to work with garden flowers. Want to come? Then a Mrs. Mowrer is going to talk about Lydia of the New Testament."

Mrs. Mowrer and Lydia might not interest Sally in the least. In fact, they may even scare her a little. But flower arranging is enticing enough to make her come in spite of herself.

The Business Meeting

Since another night out for group business purposes alone is rarely feasible, there is of necessity a formal organizational meeting every month.

The surest way to make the business less time consuming and boring is to have all recommendations and suggestions worked on by the executive committee before the meeting. Make specific suggestions. Have specific programs to present.

Here are two ways a business meeting may be conducted:

1. "I've been thinking, girls. Christmas is next month, and I guess we ought to do something. I'm not quite certain what. Do you have any ideas?" Long pause. "Remember the poor family we helped last year? Should we help them again? Or should we try something else? Or should we forget it completely because it's so close to the time and we're all so busy?" Pause. "Does anyone remember where we got the name of the poor family? Heh-heh. I guess I should have checked beforehand." Pause. "No suggestions? Then I guess we won't do anything."

2. "As you all know, Christmas is two months away. We of the board have discussed what special project we as a group can do, and we'd like to make a recommendation. We would like to get the name of another poor family from Public Assistance and make them the object of our project. In fact, the program went so well last year, we'd like to recommend that we ask for two families.

Some of us will want to give gifts to the various family members, especially the children. We would suggest that all of us put the money we would have spent on Christmas cards for each other into a fund for food for our two families. Some of us will buy a Bible, some Christian books, and some Christian records for each family. What is your reaction to our recommendation?"

The key to any business meeting is preplanning and forethought.

Refreshments

While it is always nice to have something to eat at the close of a meeting, don't fall into the I've-got-to-top-the-last-hostess trap. Have simple things—cake and coffee, pie and iced tea. Set the type of table that anyone can lay without being financially burdened.

If the group is large, share the food assignment. Let the hostess supply beverages and assign two others to each bring a cake. However you do it, let it be a financial drain on no one.

Remember that refreshments are merely the backdrop for good conversation and mingling. If supplying food becomes a problem, eating can easily be done away with without destroying the friendly atmosphere of the meeting.

4

A Program
of Helps

I, like many others, have developed a thing for plants. They are all over the house—hanging from the ceiling, reaching out from end tables, and propagating all over my kitchen window sills.

The only drawback to these fascinating green beings is that they constantly need watering. To facilitate this task, I bought one of those long-nosed plastic watering pots.

But do I, when my plants need watering, simply set my watering pot in the sink, fill it up, then leave it until my plants need watering again?

No. Obviously after I fill it, I take it from room to room and water my floral masterpieces.

A watering pot, full but sitting in the sink, does no good. It contains the life-sustaining water the plants need, but until the water is poured on them, it provides no benefit.

A Christian woman, full to bursting with good doctrine and intentions, does nothing for anyone until she reaches out. She can sit and stagnate in the sink, or she can reach out and offer practical help to troubled people.

The monthly meeting with its personal enrichment should also have a program for giving practical help--for watering needy plants.

In every group there are people in extraordinary circumstances. In every group there are people who can help the troubled ones through their difficult times. But the interesting thing about trouble is that it won't wait. There has to be an effective program for matching the needy with those able to help them before the problem situations arise, for when those times come, the troubled ones will need immediate attention.

Someone must be responsible. Someone must call people and say, "Billy Preston was hit by a car this afternoon. They don't know how seriously he is hurt yet. Will you go over Thursday and babysit for the other kids so that Bill and Sally are free to be at the hospital? Good. One more lady and we'll have the whole week covered. If Billy is going to be in for some time, I'll be back to you again."

Who should the women's group help? Only those in the church? Or the community? Or any and all?

Primary responsibility is to those within the local body of believers. James tells us that if our brother is hungry or ill-clothed, we should help him (James 2:14-17). Paul tells Timothy that if we don't provide for "our own," we are worse than infidels (I Tim. 5:8). "Bear ye one another's burdens," Paul told the Galatians. "Let us not be weary in well doing" (Gal. 6:2,9).

When we are certain we are caring for our brethren, then we can and should reach beyond. The impact on unbelievers of a group of people who care in Jesus' name is fantastic. "Love your enemies, do good to them which hate you" (Luke 6:27).

There are risks involved in reaching out to others, even to Christians. You may not be appreciated. To be blunt, so what if your help isn't esteemed? You don't help for the thanks you get. You help for Jesus' sake.

Shirley just had twins, adorable little boys she hopes will grow up to win the doubles at Wimbledon. In the meantime, Shirley is bogged down.

The women's group sent in meals the boys' first week home. Helen drives Jessica, the boys' big sister, to nursery school. Sue takes Jessica home with her every few days to give Shirley a chance to wash her hair and take a nap to prepare for the long night ahead. Josie stops in to help with the cleaning. Eileen babysits so Shirley can get to Women's Fellowship.

None of these things is in itself big, yet combined they offer much practical assistance.

Dick has cancer and is hospitalized. Jean is emotionally drained between caring for her four daughters and visiting Dick in the hospital. However, every other night she can depend on dinner being supplied by someone in her Sunday school class. Usually there is enough left over for the next night, too.

Again, it is not a lot for any one person to do, but the cumulative effect is wonderful.

With so many people needing help, we must be careful not to sit around overflowing with life-giving water. We've got to climb out of our sinks and help. We've got to examine the situation and do something—now. Maybe an older person needs his lawn mowed. Maybe a sick mother needs her house cleaned and her laundry done. Maybe a new widow needs help with her storm windows and screens.

Let's be powerful and effective in Jesus' name.

5

Extra
Possibilities

"What's for dinner, Mom?"

"Hamburger casserole with cheese, macaroni, and tomatoes in it."

"Yuk!" says one son.

"Ugh!" says the other.

"There will be no more comments like that, if you please."

We sit down to eat.

"No tomatoes on my plate," Jeff says.

"No onions on mine," Chip says.

"A little tomato is good for you, and the onion is so cooked up you can't taste it."

"Just a little then. I don't think I'm hungry."

"Me neither."

We could spend all dinner arguing over what to eat and what not to eat except for one basic rule we made when the kids were little. If you don't eat what is given to you for dinner, you may not eat any of the extras—no rolls, no dessert, no snacks, nothing to drink except water—nothing until the next meal.

We've held to that ruling—at times under duress—but we've held.

It's amazing what the promise of ice cream or a couple

23

of cookies or even sliced bananas and apples coated with a sauce of sugar, cinnamon, and lemon juice will get a child to eat.

My homemade vegetable soup goes down with fewer grumbles from Jeff if I bake old-fashioned cinnamon cake to encourage him with. Chip can stomach Brussels sprouts if they are drenched in cheese sauce. My husband can even stand to eat chicken if there is enough seasoning in the sauce to disguise its taste.

The extras are nice, no doubt about it.

In a women's program, the extras are nice too. They aren't necessary, but they add depth to the program.

Consider a book report as an extra. Introducing good Christian books to the women of your group can't help but enrich them spiritually. A biography one month, a devotional book another, a book on the Christian family, a study book, a good piece of Christian fiction; the list goes on. Circulate the reviewed books in the group.

Another extra could be a missionary report. Rarely are we as familiar with our church's missionaries as we could be. A report on a different one each month could do much to increase our knowledge. Avoid the trap of merely reading the form letters that are sent home. Always retell it in your own words.

A mini-series on a given topic might fit well in your meeting. Five minutes each month could do to developing a particular theme. One example would be how to organize a neighborhood Bible study. By the end of the series, hopefully someone will have acted and will have experiences to share.

A season of prayer could be the extra focus of your meeting. Perhaps there is a special need that calls for extra prayer. Perhaps you want to develop a caring and sharing among the group itself. Invite everyone to participate, but pressure no one.

A testimony time could be interesting in your meeting. But don't have a, "Now what has the Lord done for you recently?" followed by silence. Rather ask a specific person beforehand for a five-minute testimony. A series on how various women came to know the Lord would be fascinating.

It is also nice to have special music as part of the program. The warmth of a song can do much for that untouchable but definite part of any meeting—the mood. Select quality musicians. Or make your group a forum for future musicians by allowing children to perform.

Whatever the extra feature, it must be short and must not replace the main event. Five minutes is a good length of time.

6
Officers

Five boys stood perplexed outside my back door, each armed with a plastic bottle that squirted, each bottle filled and screaming to be emptied. The boys' quandry was purely mathematical. How could they divide five boys into two teams?

"I'll be on Chris's team," said Chip. Chris, a fourth grader, is the oldest. Chip is in third grade.

"No, I will," said Tommy, a second grader.

"No fair. I'll be on his team," said Jim, another third grader.

Not saying a word, aware that no one would consider his wishes anyway, was low-man Jeff—a first grader.

"Look," said Tommy, "I'll go with Chris. That's a fourth and a second against two thirds and a first."

"No," said Chip, unwilling to yield the choice place on Chris's team. "How about me and Jim and Chris against Tommy and Jeff?"

Tommy and Jeff looked at each other and screamed. Three big guys against them was not acceptable.

Finally Chip said, "Let's ask my mom."

I looked at the five guys.

"Why not everybody against everybody?" I asked.

"No," they chorused. "We'd get too wet that way."

As if they weren't going to get drenched if they had teams!

"Then pick a number from one to ten."

Chris picked five, Jim six, Chip four, Tommy three, and Jeff, last, two.

Fantastic. It couldn't have been better.

"Okay, guys. Even numbers on one team, odd on the other."

They lined up, Chris and Tommy facing Chip, Jim, and Jeff. It looked highly satisfactory to me—a big and a medium versus two mediums and a small. Nice balance.

They waited politely until I went back inside.

Then, "This is dumb," said Tommy who had made a similar suggestion himself not five minutes ago.

Everyone agreed with Tommy except Jeff. He couldn't afford to be particular. As far as he was concerned, any team would do.

How they solved their dilemma, I don't know. They moved away from the door and were soon squirting each other. Teams or not really didn't matter. They were all equally wet.

The boys' problem arose because no one had the authority to be team-picker. There were four highly opinionated boys (Jeff excluded), and no one would accept the others' recommendations. Lack of an authority plus confusion precluded an easy decision.

Unless jobs are spelled out in a women's group, the same uncertainty and indecision will result, to say nothing of hurt feelings and wounded egos. The organizational structure presented here calls for five officers with other positions at the discretion of the chairwoman. The officers are chairwoman, program chairwoman, secretary, treasurer, and special services chairwoman.

Before matching a person's qualifications with the specifics of each office, remember that each officer must be a woman who knows and loves the Lord. These women will set the tone for the entire organization. Their year in office should provide all members with new insights into and impetus for the Christian life. To achieve this goal, the leaders should be well acquainted with the Lord.

The executive board (the five officers mentioned plus any appointees) should be a cross section of church women, ones who have already shown an interest in the organization. A variety of backgrounds and experience not only leads to more creative programs and ideas; it also prevents the development of the clique syndrome, a certified group killer.

Part of the responsibility of each of the officers is to mingle and be friendly, especially at the monthly meetings. Move from person to person. Try to talk to everyone present. Make certain an aura of friendliness marks the group.

It may not be too strong a statement to say that this one thing—*being friendly and warm*—is the main ingredient needed to make a group click. Good speakers are important, but if they speak in a chilled atmosphere their talk is worthless. Interesting crafts are necessary, but if no friendly enthusiasm follows, craft time is wasted. *Friendliness* is the key.

I have been invited to speak to women's groups at churches unfamiliar to me. I've walked in, uncertain where I'm to go, not knowing a single soul. I've hung up my coat, smiled at the women standing around in little groups talking or looking at me, and 'been left to stand there all alone. If it weren't for the fact that I had been invited to speak and as a result knew I was *wanted*, I'd have felt foolish and hurt. Imagine how a new woman, uncertain of her welcome, must feel.

To avoid this situation, have someone who likes to smile and meet people stand by the door. She can guide lost looking people to the meeting room or introduce them to someone to talk to and sit with.

Nothing will help a women's group grow faster than being warm and welcoming. It's logical—if you have a good time, you'll come back.

Chairwoman

Besides Christian character, there are two special qualifications for the position of chairwoman. (1) She must not be a new Christian. Paul tells Timothy that the church leaders shouldn't be novices, lest they become proud (I Tim. 3:6). I think this principle applies to any position of Christian leadership. (2) It would be wise to require your chairwoman to be a church member. It indicates the extent of her commitment not only to the Lord, but also to the local work.

Though the chairwoman has many responsibilities, most of them can be filled by overseeing those under her. Any good chairwoman delegates authority.

Working on a calendar year that goes from September to September, the new chairwoman begins her tour of office by calling together her executive board in the summer. During these planning sessions the year's theme is selected, speakers for the year are chosen, craft demonstrators are picked, and hostesses for the coming year are listed.

After the speakers are chosen, the chairwoman and program chairwoman present the list and some pertinent biographical information to the church board for its approval.

By the end of August, a good chairwoman will have the September through June meetings planned and a program of events printed and distributed to all interested women.

Monthly, the chairwoman either leads the meeting herself or selects in advance someone to lead it for her. She may appoint someone to hostess the guest speaker for the evening. She plans carefully and in detail the order of events for the evening and sees to their discharge.

Program Chairwoman

Like the chairwoman, the program chairwoman shouldn't be a novice. Selecting speakers calls for a certain degree of spiritual maturity and discernment that develop only with time and training. Church membership is discretionary.

The primary responsibility of the program chairwoman is, obviously, to plan the year's program. This means finding and contacting speakers and craft demonstrators. It is a big responsibility, but if done right, it is largely finished by September 1.

When a speaker or craft person is called and invited, describe as fully as possible your organization, its year's theme, and the particular topic you would like her or him to discuss. Be specific on date, time, and place. Two weeks before each meeting call the speaker and craft person to confirm the evening to avoid date confusion and time discrepancies.

Once a pastoral candidate appeared for his Sunday morning service at 12:25, arriving as we were leaving. Somehow he had mistaken the street address for the time. We were not impressed.

A confirming call is to avoid such mistakes.

Secretary

The secretary keeps accurate records of all business of the organization. She takes minutes at general meetings and executive meetings. She is responsible for the correspondence of the group, excluding speaker contacts. She should also write thank you notes to all speakers and craft demonstrators within a week of their visit.

Treasurer

A treasurer must keep careful financial records for the women's group. The larger the group becomes, the more important this becomes. All monies received are recorded and all monies spent should be carefully noted and paid by check for accuracy.

The church board may require a financial statement from the women's group. If so, it is the treasurer's responsibility to furnish it.

Special Services Chairwoman

The program of practical helps falls under the auspices of special services as does planning a covered dish dinner or a family picnic. Anything extra the group plans is under the overseership of this person. She can delegate responsibility as she feels necessary.

Special services is the type of job that's as big or little as the chairwoman chooses to make it. With some thought, this job can have a far-reaching effect, especially in its ministry of practical helps.

7

Special
Programs

Christmas

There is such a special feeling about Christmas that a topical program seems necessary. To make the program unusual, how about: (1) a musical evening, (2) a dramatic reading, or (3) a sharing of "how we make Christmas special at our house."

Crafts can range from making advent wreaths to homemade gifts to Christmas foods or decorations.

Refreshments can be a holiday smorgasbord where everyone brings a favorite dessert, or a cookie exchange where each woman brings one dozen to be eaten and one dozen to be exchanged and taken home.

May Banquet

The specialty speaker of the year—one who will make the evening spiritually exciting—is invited for this night. If necessary, ask the church board to underwrite the expenses. The banquet may be catered, be potluck, or be a mother-daughter affair served by the men. If it is the latter, choose the speaker with the little ones in mind.

Make the evening special with decorations. Also consider where you will eat. A progressive dinner might be fun. (Near us there is a county park with a lovely old mansion that can be rented for a nominal fee by church and civic groups. The old ballroom can be set with tables, and a little kitchen has been added on one end. It's an elegant setting that makes the whole evening unique.)

A special craft program such as a fashion show or wedding gowns down Memory Lane show, or a plant party by a local greenhouse add luster to the evening.

Family Picnic

Before the group adjourns for the summer, a picnic is great fun. Late spring when the weather is warming up is just right for a time of fellowship.

Select the site for your picnic carefully. A park with a pavilion and play things or a farm with a lot of open space is good. Nothing is worse than scores of people, a good percentage of them exuberant children, in cramped quarters.

Have some hours of the day structured, some free. Appoint an athletic director. (Husbands come in handy here.) Plan group games that everybody, even the kids, can play. Relays are especially good. Have a treasure hunt or a softball game. Pit the moms against the dads in an egg toss.

In short, laugh and play together. Informal times like a picnic do wonderful things for a group. Jeans and dirty hands help make people less reserved. Sweating together on a softball team makes friends much more quickly than sitting together in the same pew Sunday mornings.

The easiest plan for dinner is for each to bring his own. Then there is no worrying over how many are coming. Provide a fireplace and let each family cook its own meat.

For a fun dessert, make homemade ice cream. The kids will think it's wonderful. Or pop popcorn over the campfire. Or toast marshmallows.

Plan a hymn-sing. Have a few testimonies. Be casual and low-key. Have fun.

✦ 8 ✦

Five Years of
Meeting Plans

The programs presented here run on an organizational year of September to June. July and August are free due to the difficulties presented by complicated summer schedules.

The September meeting that begins each year has a summary topic that introduces the year's theme.

Each calendar has been prepared with three specialty programs—in December, May, and June. These three meetings need not be faithful to the year's theme.

Year 1: God's Creative Woman

"She worketh willingly with her hands"
(Prov. 31:13).

PURPOSE: to help develop our God-given talents in the arena of our daily lives.

SEPTEMBER
Creative Prayer Life
"The effectual fervent prayer of a righteous man availeth much" (James 5:16b).
The purpose of this theme is to enrich personal prayer experience. Consider using a book review of a recent or classic book on prayer, a sharing time of prayer experiences and patterns by the members, a presentation and discussion on the structure of prayer, or readings of classic prayers. Prayer study guides you may want to use are: *Alive to God Through Prayer*, Donald E. Demaray; *Power Through Prayer*, E. M. Bounds; *You Can Pray Effectively*, William J. Krutza. All are published by Baker Book House and are available at your local Christian bookstore.

OCTOBER
Creative Cookery
"Give us this day our daily bread" (Matt. 6:11).
This program is centered on making meals and mealtimes profitable for the Lord. You may want to invite a home economist to speak to your group on economical yet nutritious meal planning or ask the women to bring recipes for basic and economical dishes. Discuss methods of

holding mealtime devotions and ways to get children involved in mealtime activities.

NOVEMBER
Flowers and Things
"The grass withereth, the flower fadeth: but the word of our God shall stand for ever" (Isa. 40:8).

Share ideas and suggestions for making homes warm and alive with physical and spiritual beauty. You may want to ask someone to give a demonstration on flower arranging, a presentation on interior decorating, or a talk on organizing family devotions. Review *Hidden Art* by Edith Schaeffer (Tyndale).

DECEMBER
Holiday Hostessing
"Use hospitality one to another without grudging" (I Peter 4:9).

Stress that we are ministers through our hospitality. It is not important to impress guests with expensive spreads of food and elaborate decorations during the holiday season. What is important is that we show Christ's love to our guests through our lives. The response of Mary and Martha to the visit of Jesus sets an example of the way we should treat our guests. Ask the women to bring a homemade Christmas ornament and instructions for making it or a batch of Christmas cookies and the recipe to exchange. Plan to make a family advent calendar or advent wreath. Review *Open Heart, Open Home* by Karen Burton Mains (Cook).

JANUARY
Creative Marriage

"Wives, submit yourselves unto your own husbands, as unto the Lord" (Eph. 5:22).

This program is designed to help women make their marriage relationships as satisfying and delightful as God intended. You may want to have a study centered on one of the many new books written on Christian marriage, to discuss the woman's role as directed in Ephesians 5:22, or to examine the marriages of couples in the Bible. Review *Heaven Help the Home* by Howard Hendricks (Victor), *His Stubborn Love* by Joyce Landorf (Zondervan), or *Christian Living in the Home* by Jay E. Adams (Baker).

FEBRUARY
Creative Singleness

"Brethren, let every man, wherein he is called, therein abide with God" (I Cor. 7:24).

This month's program is designed to show how single women can live joyful and fulfilling Christian lives. Organize a discussion using for panelists a widow who has successfully coped with living completely alone, a widow who is raising children, and a single woman who has never been married. Ask the other women to prepare questions for the panelists. You may want to ask someone to present a book review, perhaps of *Alone* by Katie F. Wiebe (Tyndale) or *Your Half of the Apple* by Gini Andrews (Zondervan).

MARCH
Creative Mothering
"Her children rise up, and call her blessed" (Prov. 31:28a).
Learning to be a more effective Christian mother is this month's theme. Here again is a prime opportunity to invite a guest speaker or to give a book review. Some suggestions for book reviews are *What They Did Right* by Virginia Hearn (Tyndale), *Hide and Seek* by James Dobson (Revell), or *Mom, Take Time* by Pat Baker (Baker). You may want to hold a discussion on the problems of today's children and offer some solutions for their dilemmas. A school counselor or child psychologist could enlighten you on the problems facing children outside the home. Plan craft time around hobbies that parents can share with their children.

APRIL
Creative Recreation
"And he said unto them, Come ye yourselves apart into a desert place, and rest awhile" (Mark 6:31a).
Spring is the time for families to get outside to relax and play together. Use this meeting to suggest trips to take and things to see and do together. Ask each woman to compile a list of short trips she has taken with her family and things her family does to relax together. Share these with each other. Invite someone involved in a camp or summer ministry to speak.

MAY
Banquet

JUNE
Picnic

Year 2: SOS—Serving Our Savior

"And whatsoever ye do in word or deed, do all in the name of the Lord Jesus, giving thanks to God and the Father by him" (Col. 3:17).

PURPOSE: to explore service opportunities for the Christian woman outside her family.

SEPTEMBER
Called to Serve
"For we are his workmanship, created in Christ Jesus unto good works, which God hath before ordained that we should walk in them" (Eph. 2:10).

God has a job for *every* woman to do. No matter how limited a person's talents may seem, if they are given to God, He will use them to bless someone. To show the importance of not wasting our talents, you may want to read the story of the servants and the talents from Matthew 25:14-30. Before the meeting make a list of jobs that women can do for their friends, church, community, missions, hospitals, etc. Make enough copies so that each woman may have one. Challenge each woman to do the good works the Lord has for her. At craft time make gifts for hospital or nursing home patients or for missions.

OCTOBER
Teaching
"Come, ye children, hearken unto me: I will teach you the fear of the Lord" (Ps. 34:11).

According to II Timothy 4:2 Christians should be prepared at all times to share with others the truth of the

Scriptures. Suggest methods for teaching your children God's Word at home and methods for witnessing to other adults. Enlist the help of a master teacher or psychologist to give a demonstration/lecture on how parents teach *without* words (body language, physical environment). Remind everyone that God's Word can be shared with unconverted adults via greeting cards, letters, Christian books, kind deeds, and Christian conversation. Stress the fact that we must *learn* the Word before we can *teach* others.

NOVEMBER
Music

"Speaking to yourselves in psalms and hymns and spiritual songs, singing and making melody in your heart to the Lord" (Eph. 5:19).

This month's program theme stresses the need for all Christians, not musicians only, to make use of music. Ask musically talented women or some of the members' children to perform at your meeting. Enlist the services of your choir director or organist to give members a list of good records and tapes that would provide a good music library for a family. As a group, learn one or two new songs, either contemporary or classic.

DECEMBER
Special Christmas Program

JANUARY
Children's Work
"But Jesus said, Suffer little children, and forbid them not, to come unto me; for of such is the kingdom of heaven" (Matt. 19:14).

Reaching children for Christ through neighborhood kids' clubs or on a one-to-one basis is the theme for this meeting. Invite your church's youth pastor or someone who has started a kids' club to give specific instructions for starting such a project. Encourage the members to begin their own clubs. Stress the ministry of all parents not only to their children, but to their children's friends.

FEBRUARY
Bible Studies
"Study to shew thyself approved unto God, a workman that needeth not to be ashamed, rightly dividing the word of truth" (II Tim. 2:15).

Whether they are teachers, students, or pew-sitters, all Christians should be studying and sharing God's Word. Have someone give a presentation on methods for daily Bible reading. Pass out tracts that have a schedule of daily Scripture readings whereby a person can complete reading the Bible in one year. As a group, discuss or review a variety of devotional guides. Share experiences gathered from women's Bible study groups, especially neighborhood studies. Encourage each other to consider the ministry of such study groups, whether as teacher, hostess, or babysitter.

MARCH
Books
"Seek ye out of the book of the Lord, and read" (Isa. 34:16).

Reading and sharing books is a ministry. Have each of the women bring a favorite Christian book to exchange and present a brief review of it. If your members wouldn't respond to such a suggestion, with the help of the church librarian, select a number of good books, give a synopsis of several, and offer them to the women to read. Encourage the sharing of exciting Christian literature with unchurched neighbors and friends.

APRIL
Helps
"As we have therefore opportunity, let us do good to all men, especially unto them who are of the household of faith" (Gal. 6:10).

The theme for this springtime meeting is doing things for others out of love for them. Since this is the Easter season, you may want to study the story of Christ's death, the ultimate gift of love. Ask the women to relate incidents that demonstrate "love deeds." Brainstorm on ways your group can show love in your local situation. Be extremely practical.

MAY
Banquet

JUNE
Picnic

Year 3: Winsome Women

"Favour is deceitful and beauty is vain, but a woman who feareth the Lord, she shall be praised" (Prov. 31:30).

PURPOSE: to learn lessons for our lives by studying women of the Bible.

SEPTEMBER
The Epitome

"Many daughters have done virtuously, but thou excellest them all" (Prov. 31:29).

Encouraging women to pattern their lives after Christ's is this month's program theme. Of course not one of us is a perfect wife or mother, but if we search out God's will and follow it, we will become what God wants us to be. Read about the woman of Proverbs 31:10-31 to see what characteristics a godly wife and mother will have. Beforehand assign one verse to each member to think about, research, and draw practical lessons from. Let each participant give a short report. For a study guide see my *WIFE: Mate, Mother, Me* (Baker).

OCTOBER
Sarah

"Through faith also Sara herself received strength to conceive seed, and was delivered of a child when she was past age, because she judged him faithful who had promised" (Heb. 11:11).

Our subject this month is Abraham's wife Sarah. Sarah at first laughed at the thought of having a child in her old

48

age, but knowing that her God always kept His promises,* she put her faith in Him and waited. God honored Sarah's faith by giving her Isaac. We should build our faith in God as Sarah did by asking ourselves the question God asked her: "Is any thing too hard for the Lord?" (Gen. 18:14).

NOVEMBER
Ruth
"And Ruth said, Intreat me not to leave thee, . . . thy people shall be my people, and thy God my God" (Ruth 1:16).

A book of the Bible was devoted to the life story of this month's featured woman, Ruth. Unlike many mother-in-law/daughter-in-law relationships today, Ruth and her mother-in-law had a strong love for each other. Even after Ruth's husband died, Ruth stood by her mother-in-law and cared for her despite persecution from outsiders. Use this meeting as a time to rid ourselves of possible bitter feelings towards in-laws. Several good plays and readings on the Book of Ruth are available. Enlist the help of several volunteers to read through or present a play from one of these.

DECEMBER
Mary, the Mother of Jesus
"And Mary said, Behold the handmaid of the Lord; be it unto me according to thy word. . . . And Mary said, My soul doth magnify the Lord" (Luke 1:38, 46).

The fruit of obedience to God is the lesson we learn from this month's subject. If God gave some women today the commission He gave Mary—bearing and raising His

Son—they would refuse. Not many would want to face the gossip and reproach that Mary faced. God asks His Christian women to do much simpler things today, yet many refuse. Challenge each woman to be willing to be the Lord's handmaid. Since this is the Christmas season, you have a large choice of program ideas. Make up some gift baskets for the needy and carol as you go from house to house to deliver the baskets. Or make gifts for needy children, the elderly, and the homebound.

JANUARY
Hannah

"And Hannah prayed and said, My heart rejoiceth in the Lord . . ." (I Sam. 2:1).

Another Old Testament woman of great faith was Hannah. Like Abraham's wife Sarah, Hannah was barren, yet by a miracle of God, she gave birth to a son. Hannah dedicated her son Samuel to service in God's temple even before he was conceived. Stress the point throughout this month's meeting that we should dedicate our children to God, pray for them, and teach them God's Word. Ask some of the older women with grown children to testify to the truth of Proverbs 22:6—"Train up a child in the way he should go: and when he is old, he will not depart from it." Discuss sections of *Christian Child-rearing and Personality Development* by Paul Meier (Baker) or *How to Raise Your Children for Christ* by Andrew Murray (Bethany Fellowship). A child psychologist who is a Christian could share insights on child-raising with the members.

FEBRUARY
Esther

"And Esther obtained favour in the sight of all them that looked upon her" (Esther 2:15).

Queen Esther was a queen not only by title, but also by virtue. Risking her life, she went before the king with a petition that he save her people, the Jews. Her attitude was, "If I perish, I perish." She wanted to do her best for her fellowmen and for God no matter what the cost. That is the attitude with which we should face each day. We should do our best to serve our family, friends, community, and Lord. Then we, like Esther, will be favored by all.

This month accent outward as well as inward beauty. Invite someone to demonstrate the proper use of cosmetics, present figure-flattering clothing fashions, or demonstrate a daily exercise plan. Review *Fragrance of Beauty* by Joyce Landorf (Pyramid).

MARCH
Mary and Martha

"Now Jesus loved Martha, and her sister [Mary], and Lazarus" (John 11:5).

From the New Testament sisters Mary and Martha, we can learn a lesson in setting priorities. Read Luke 10:38-42. Martha had her mind set on fixing a fancy dinner for Christ, and Mary had her mind set on anointing and worshiping Him. Christ told the sisters that what Mary was doing was of greater benefit. Let this meeting be a time of evaluating our motives for service. Review *You and Your Thoughts* by Earl Radmacher (Tyndale).

APRIL
Lydia

"And a certain woman named Lydia, . . . whose heart the Lord opened . . ." (Acts 16:14).

A widowed Christian businesswoman named Lydia owned a fabric-dyeing business in Philippi during the apostle Paul's time. But unlike many businesswomen, Lydia did not make her work her top priority in life—she put God first. Her elegant house was always open for fellowship, worship services, and Bible study. Invite a few successful businesswomen to share their testimonies at your meeting. You may want them to form a panel for a discussion.

MAY
Banquet

JUNE
Picnic

Year 4: All One Body We

"What? know ye not that your body is the temple of the Holy Ghost which is in you, which ye have of God, and ye are not your own? For ye are bought with a price: therefore glorify God in your body . . ." (I Cor. 6:19, 20).

PURPOSE: to emphasize our total commitment to God as seen in each body member.

SEPTEMBER
The Body of Christ
"For as the body is one and hath many members, and all the members of that one body, being many, are one body: so also is Christ" (I Cor. 12:12).

Use the September meeting to challenge each woman to be used by God as a member of the body of Christ. Without each person doing her God-given part, the body, the church, can't function at peak efficiency. Some jobs, such as teaching, are highly visible, however, many jobs, such as praying, are not visible. Whatever we do, we need each other just as the eyes need the ears and the feet need the hands.

OCTOBER
Our Feet
"He brought me up also out of an horrible pit, out of the miry clay, and set my feet upon a rock" (Ps. 40:2).

Zero in on the implication that our feet should follow

Christ. A movie or firsthand account of someone in full-time Christian work could illustrate this. Try to find someone in your local area who serves with dedication in an unusual way (directs a rest home, children's home, youth home) and needs volunteers to assist in specific areas.

NOVEMBER
A Sound Mind
"For God hath not given us the spirit of fear; but of power, and of love, and of a sound mind" (II Tim. 1:7).

Anxiety, fear, and guilt often torment Christians. Examine the marvelous freeing aspect of salvation. Invite someone who has felt the burden-lifting power of Christ to share her testimony. Hear a Christian counselor or psychologist.

DECEMBER
Christmas Program

JANUARY
Let My Mouth Speak
"Of the abundance of the heart his mouth speaketh" (Luke 6:45).

Have a practical mini-workshop on how to witness. Invite the head of the church evangelism team to demonstrate the do's and don't's of sharing the gospel. Panel discussions and small discussion groups could work well here, as could role playing.

FEBRUARY
Ears to Hear
"He who hath ears to hear, let him hear" (Matt. 13:9).

Have three or four members work out choral readings of some favorite psalms and/or other Bible passages as an effective way to discover new riches in Scripture. Schedule a Christian psychologist or social worker to speak on the topic: "How to Be a Good Listener." Perhaps an ear specialist can speak on hearing disabilities in children and adults, or a teacher of the deaf can share potential church ministries to this group. An alternative emphasis could be the deafness of people to the voice of God.

MARCH
Hands, the Doers
"Whatsoever thy hand findeth to do, do it with all thy might" (Eccles. 9:10).

Stress the need for total commitment to each task, whether it is making dinner for the family or painting a picture to be gallery-hung. Discuss practical services the hands can perform for the church family. These services could include ministering to single mothers or senior shut-ins, providing emergency baby sitting and food supply, or serving as volunteer drivers. Hands soothe the troubled and care for the needy.

APRIL
Eyes, the Light of the Body
"The light of the body is the eye; therefore when the eye is single, thy whole body also is full of light" (Luke 11:34).

Use this month to develop "new eyes" to see beauty not

only in nature, but also in people. A nature slide presentation by a local museum staff member; a trip to a nearby nature center, local nursery, or floral garden; or a lecture by a local naturalist could serve to develop an awareness of nature. Perhaps a staff member of a local Family Services Association could give clues on recognizing the "beauty" of people and give the members tips on developing their own "beautiful personalities." The purpose, of course, is to use this new awareness as a springboard of praise to the One who created all things.

MAY
Banquet

JUNE
Picnic

Year 5: So Should We Be

"Be ye therefore perfect, even as your Father which is in heaven is perfect" (Matt. 5:48).

PURPOSE: to explore the qualities that should be the hallmarks of our Christian lives.

SEPTEMBER
The Christian's Character

"But the fruit of the Spirit is love, joy, peace, longsuffering, gentleness, goodness, faith, meekness, temperance; against such there is no law" (Gal. 5:22, 23).

At this first meeting of the new year stress the point that Christian qualities are called "fruit" and therefore should grow as fruit grows. Ask nine women to each talk on one of the fruits of the Spirit. Encourage the women to use examples of people in the Bible who possessed these qualities.

OCTOBER
A Gracious Woman

"A gracious woman retaineth honour" (Prov. 11:16).
Plan a lively, open discussion by all the members on "Graciousness is. . . ." After exploring the dictionary definitions, consult good commentaries, and then make some practical applications on just what graciousness is. You may want to have a chalkboard to list suggestions from the audience.

NOVEMBER
A Wise Woman
*"Every wise woman buildeth her house: but the foolish
one plucketh it down with her hands" (Prov. 14:1).*

A woman who wisely builds (manages) her house (hold)
must have an abundance of source books and advisors.
Consult your church librarian for a list of worthwhile
books on homemaking, marriage, budgeting, and child-
raising. Using this as background, have different people
summarize tips and advice in specific areas (finance, nutri-
tion, minor home repairs, etc.). Stress that this must not
be a general coverage of a broad subject but should be
helpful tidbits in a special area. Review *What Husbands
Wish Their Wives Knew About Money* by Larry
Burkett (Victor) or *Living on Less and Liking It* by Maxine
Hancock (Moody).

DECEMBER
A Christmas Program

JANUARY
A Faith-filled Woman
*"Then Jesus answered and said to her, O woman, great is
thy faith . . ." (Matt. 15:28).*

While He walked the earth Jesus performed many
miracles for people who were in dire need of His help.
He is the same today as He was then and continues to
perform miracles for people in need. Use this meeting as
a time of faith building. Study some of the miracles of the
Bible, then ask the women to testify of miracles Christ
has performed in their lives.

FEBRUARY
A Woman of Good Works
". . . this woman was full of good works and almsdeeds which she did" (Acts 9:36).

According to James 2:17, faith without works is dead. Christ expects Christian women to be doers and to have a reputation for good works. Challenge each woman to consider her reputation. Can people tell she is a Christian by what she does and how she does it? Ask three or four women to give short biographies of biblical or contemporary Christian women who were/are "full of good works."

MARCH
A Chosen Woman
"The elder unto the elect lady and her children, whom I love in the truth; and not I only, but also all they that have known the truth" (II John 1).

Get every woman involved in your March meeting by choosing each one to do something different. Plan a progressive dinner and have two or three women work on each course (this depends on the size of your group). Stress that each woman is important because she is "chosen" to do her part—if she fails to prepare her portion of the meal, all will miss it. Be sure to plan a simple dinner route so that you can move from house to house quickly. Ask one woman to lead devotions, stressing that we are each chosen, first for salvation, then for service.

59

APRIL
A Virtuous Woman
"A virtuous woman is a crown to her husband: but she that maketh ashamed is as rottenness in his bones" (Prov. 12:4).
Invite a Christian psychologist to talk to your group on woman as man's helpmeet. Many women may be unaware that they are doing or saying things that tear their husbands down rather than build them up. This again is an opportunity to recognize outward beauty as the complement to inner beauty. Have a cosmetic demonstration, spring fashion show, or daily exercise plan presentation.

MAY
Banquet

JUNE
Picnic

Crafts

Make certain a craft person realizes she is to do a demonstration. Give her fifteen minutes to demonstrate. Pay her for her time and effort, even if it's only five dollars.

Advent wreaths
applique
cake decorating
candle making
canning and preserving
ceramics
cooking
crewel
decoupage
dough art
drapedolls
drying flowers

embroidery
flower arranging
gardening
hooking
macrame
painting
photography
pine cone possibilities
quilling
stained glass
stitchery
wreaths